START THE CONVERSATION

52

QUESTIONS

FOR RELATIONSHIPS

**LEARN MORE ABOUT YOUR RELATIONSHIP
ONE QUESTION AT A TIME**

hatherleigh
Improve your life. Change your world.

Hatherleigh Press is committed to preserving
and protecting the natural resources of the earth.
Environmentally responsible and sustainable practices
are embraced within the company's
mission statement.
Visit us at www.hatherleighpress.com and register online
for free offers, discounts, special events,
and more.

52 Questions for a Better Relationship
Text copyright © 2017 Travis Hellstrom

Library of Congress Cataloging-in-Publication Data is available upon request.
ISBN: 978-1-57826-691-3

Printed in the United States
10 9 8 7 6 5 4 3 2 1

DEDICATION

This book is dedicated to the love of my life—my wife, Tunga, who is always up for an adventure; and to all the wonderful people in our lives who show us what love is every day.

CONTENTS

INTRODUCTION

This simple book is designed to help you build a stronger relationship with someone you love.

These questions are meant to help you start a great conversation, reconnect with who you really are, learn more about yourself and your partner, and deepen relationships with people you love. They are also meant to complement my other books, *52 Questions for a Better Friendship* and *52 Questions for a Happy Family*.

You will find that some questions are categorized as "Light", some are "Fun", and some are "Deep". I've used these categories so you can easily flip through the book and see the type of question on the top of the page. No matter which kind of question you encounter, I hope all of them are fun for you. I also left blank space to the left of each question for you to add notes and thoughts from your conversations.

I hope you enjoy this book, whether you are asking one question a week (which will conveniently take you exactly one year) or just jumping in and asking them whenever you like.

Good luck and have fun!

Travis

I would not wish any companion in the world but you.

Shakespeare

52 QUESTIONS

What recharges your batteries?

What makes you feel powerful?

Given the choice of anyone in the world, whom would you want as a dinner guest?

What's your favorite season, and why?

Before making a telephone call, do you ever rehearse what you are going to say? Why?

fun

What would be a "perfect" day for you?

Would you like to be famous? In what way?

What's your "love language"?

If you're not sure, take this free quiz:
www.travishellstrom.com/love-
languages

What's your idea of a perfect birthday dinner?

What are two
of your favorite
romantic songs?

deep

What do you think is holding me back?

Do you have a secret
hunch about how
you will die?

light

What three things do
we have in common?

light

For what in your life do you feel most grateful?

If you could change one thing about the way you were raised, what would it be?

deep

Take four minutes
and tell your life
story in as much
detail as possible.

fun

If you could wake up and have gained any one quality or ability, what would it be?

fun

If a crystal ball could tell you the truth about anything, what would you want to know?

What's one of my qualities that you wish you could have?

deep

Is there anything
you've dreamed
of doing for a
long time?

What do you think
I could be doing to
be happier?

fun

What is one thing you are passionate about right now?

What is one of
the greatest
accomplishments
of your life?

What's your favorite
type of cake?

deep

What do you
value most in a
relationship?

fun

What are two of your favorite love movies?

See "24 Great Love Movies" in the Resources section of this book for some ideas.

What's one of your most treasured memories?

light

What is your guilty pleasure?

light

What's your fondest memory of us?

Do you remember
when you first
saw me?

What was your first
impression of me?

If you knew you were going to die one year from today, would you change anything about the way you are living?

What does a healthy relationship mean to you?

What roles do love and affection play in your life?

What are five of my positive characteristics?

(Share five each.)

How close is your family? Do you feel your childhood was happier than most people's?

How do you feel about your relationship with your mother?

What's something fun you'd like to be doing 10 years from now?

fun

Would you be up for picking a weekly date night idea from a jar?

If yes, see "52 Fun Date Night Ideas" in the Resources section of this book.

fun

What kind of a relationship did you dream of having when you were 16?

fun

What is one of the times when we had the most fun together?

fun

If you could live anywhere for six months, where would you want to live?

What are three of
your favorite things
about me?

What's one important thing I should know about you?

What's the funniest thing that's ever happened to you?

What's something I
could help you with?

light

What do you miss most about being a child?

If you died tonight,
what would you
most regret
not having told
someone?

What's something that I could teach you to help you live a better life?

What's something I
could do that would
probably help
me live an extra
10 years?

Your house is on fire. Your loved ones and pets are fine, what one thing do you save?

fun

What's something weird or funny you like to do that I don't know about?

The art and science of asking questions is the source of all knowledge.

Thomas Berger

RESOURCES

MAKE THE QUESTIONS A GAME

Over the years, I have had the pleasure of testing these questions out on lots of my family and friends. In this section you'll find some suggestions and examples on how to use the questions in this book.

FOLLOW THE LEADER
Choose a group leader or "game host" to help lead the discussion and remember, there are no right or wrong answers and no time limit.

HOT POTATO
Pass the book to a new "answerer". The answerer flips to a random question in the book and reads it aloud to the group. Then the answerer shares their response. If they have difficulty with the question, anyone else is welcome to contribute. After the first question is discussed, pass the book and move

on to the next person who is now the new answerer.

ONE TO ONE

A new reader holds the book and picks a question or flips to a random page in the book. The reader chooses someone who they would like to have answer the question and reads the question to them. They share their answer with the group.

CHANGELING

A new reader holds the book and picks a question or flips to a random page in the book. The reader reads or alters a question. Each question is simply a starting point. The reader can take it in any direction they desire. The most important thing is to have fun!

52 FUN DATE NIGHT IDEAS

(from www.travishellstrom.com/date-night)

1. Plan a picnic
2. Take a mini road trip
3. Go snowshoeing
4. Dinner and a movie
5. Drive-in movie
6. Go bowling
7. Play a kids game
8. Walk to dinner
9. Go apple picking
10. Stargaze
11. Take the scenic route home
12. Visit a farmer's market
13. Sign up for a race
14. Go to a sports game
15. Visit a plant nursery
16. Go kayaking

17. OMake a bucket list
18. Attend a book reading
19. Give DIY massages
20. Plan a long sleep-in
21. Explore a winery
22. Wander a bookstore
23. Play with puppies
24. Take a surprise trip
25. Sleep by a fireplace
26. Find a local swimming hole
27. Play an outdoor sport
28. Go pottery painting
29. Go thrift shopping
30. Go on a dinner cruise
31. Take a brewery tour
32. Discover a museum
33. Act like a tourist
34. Visit a flea market
35. Have a game night
36. Go to the opera
37. Visit a gourmet grocery store
38. Go on a hike
39. Go to a dinner party
40. Visit a coffee shop
41. Go to a county fair
42. Take a new class
43. Learn a new dance

44. Go to a trivia night
45. Host a fondue night
46. Volunteer together
47. Try a fitness class
48. Head to the spa
49. Get extra sex ed
50. See a morning matinee
51. Find an art gallery
52. Drive without a destination

24 GREAT LOVE MOVIES

1. *About Time*
2. *The Notebook*
3. *WALL-E*
4. *Enchanted*
5. *Casablanca*
6. *Dirty Dancing*
7. *Love Actually*
8. *P.S. I Love You*
9. *Groundhog's Day*
10. *When Harry Met Sally*
11. *Breakfast at Tiffany's*
12. *Back to the Future*
13. *Pretty Woman*
14. *Roman Holiday*
15. *Amelie*
16. *Avatar*
17. *Say Anything*
18. *Stardust*
19. *Notting Hill*

20. *Grease*
21. *The Princess Bride*
22. *Sleepless in Seattle*
23. *Slumdog Millionaire*
24. *Bridge to Terabithia*

ABOUT THE AUTHOR

Travis Hellstrom is an optimist, husband, professor and author who helps people dream big and expand their influence. He is a Returned Peace Corps Volunteer and Founder of Advance Humanity. He is the author of *The Peace Corps Volunteer's Handbook* and The *Dalai Lama Book of Quotes*. To read more from Travis, visit www.travishellstrom.com.